# By God's Grace -Still Surviving

**Books Academy LLC**
5900 Balcones Drive Suite 100
Austin, Texas 78731
Hotline: (254) 800-1183

**Contact the Author at:**
J C V Communications
Box 566
Fremont, OH 43420
drgenav@drgenav.com
www.bygodsgrace.net
419-913-9139

Ordering Information:
Quantity sales. Special discounts are available on quantity purchases by corporations, associations, and others. For details, contact the publisher at the address above.

Printed in the United States of America.

| ISBN-13: | Softcover | 978-1-964929-33-0 |
| --- | --- | --- |
| | eBook | 978-1-964929-34-7 |

Library of Congress Control Number:   2024919440

# By God's Grace - Still Surviving

Dr. Regina Vincent-Williams

BOOKS ACADEMY
LEARNING LIFE FROM EVERY PAGE

**All art is autobiographical. The pearl is the oyster's autobiography.**

**— Federico Fellini**

*Pearls symbolize wisdom acquired through experience. They are believed to attract wealth and luck as well as offer protection. Known for their calming effect, pearls can balance one's karma, strengthen relationships, and keep children safe. The pearl is also said to symbolize the purity, generosity, integrity, and loyalty of its wearer.*

# Contents

# When Between
# a Rock and a Very Hard Place

For I know the plans I have for you, declares the Lord, plans to prosper
you, and not to harm you, plans to give you hope and a future.
Jeremiah 29:11


Be still and know that I am God. Psalm 46:10

Faith, hope, love – the greatest of these is love. I Corinthians 13:13

And we know all things work together for good to them that love God,
to them who are the called according to His purpose. Romans 8:28


Not by might nor by power, but by my Spirit. Zechariah 4:6

All things are possible to those who believe. Mark 9:23.

Call those things which be not as though they were. Romans 4:17

# Introduction

## If I Am Surviving, So Will You

I have been encouraged a number of times to write a book about my colorful, busy as ever, adventurous life. I am not much of a swimmer, but I have gone whitewater rafting several times. I hopped on a jet-ski once with my granddaughter – that was fun. I have taken the very narrow, close quarters hike to get to the top of one of the pyramids in Egypt. I lived and worked for two years in Antigua. I have parasailed, gone deep-sea fishing in Costa Rica, and snowmobiling in Colorado. Maybe an autobiography would be an interesting reflection project one day.

I am a poet. Quite frankly, I have never given much thought to putting pen to paper specifically for an autobiography, short stories or a novel. Although yes I have completed a couple of short stories for my grandchildren. But an autobiography? That sounds very, very challenging. However, I must admit my poetry is autobiographical. I have been in denial about that but this time I am owning up to me. Owning up to who I am. What and who I have become – thanks to God. And somewhat who I am to others in my life. Thanks to God. I have held and played so many roles.

And all in all, I have enjoyed - no - loved being me. How could I not enjoy being me? God created me. He created me in His image to love people. To love myself with joy. But it was only recently that I understood what self-love and self-care mean. Scarlett Johannson, wrote: "I'm just a big believer in 'you must love yourself before you can love anybody else' and I think for me that breeds the most inspired relationships." This book on survival is really about relationships of all kinds. Especially… love.

As for writing an autobiography, By God's Grace…. Still Surviving is a start. This is very, very personal and at the same time a very, very universal poetic account of my life. I started writing and planning the book in 2018 as a celebration of the 30th anniversary of my very first book, titled Surviving Life Between a Rock and a Very Hard Place. Time flies, believe me. For anyone hoping to tell your story in your own book, it is not so important how, where or why you start. The best advice I can offer is when! "When?" you ask. "Yes, Now!!'

In the 1988 publication I was in denial about how much of my personal life I wanted shared so publicly. At the time, my 17-year marriage was ending. The proverbial writing was clearly on the wall. As a disclaimer, I must warn you, my directness and honesty are brutal. Poetry is personal. But like life, poetry is universal. Issues and challenges are universal. I can say that I have now read many more books, articles, and blogs on marriage and relationships today in an effort to save relationships. To survive relationships. To give as much joy as I get – or more!

Thankful to the utmost am I that God has led me through many trials and tribulations, hills and valleys, good times and bad times (which are said to make us stronger) until I am who I am today: Strong, resilient, a fighter, a non-give-upper for the most part, thinking, analytical, sometimes cynical, and almost always, "in search of something" human being/Child of God! I am as one poem will read – Desperately Seeking… knowledge, understanding, peace, and above all else - a true relationship with the Creator.

When you reach this age (yes, this golden senior age), you no longer want distrust, fussing, arguments, cheating, disappointments, doubt or frivolity. This is a good age. This is my time for peace. My time for joy. Writing brings me joy. Christ reminds me of the joy I deserve. "I came that you might have joy and have it more abundantly." John 10:10. I believe this! The mere fact that you are reading this book probably suggests that you desire that same joy, peace, love and happiness.

So By God's Grace – Still Surviving is different from other books I have done. This book is clearly dedicated to my determined and renewed ambition to seek and find that joy and peace that surpasses all understanding. I have had this joy before. This joy has been described in many songs – gospel and secular: This joy I have the world didn't give it and the world can't take it away. Joy, Joy, God's Great Joy (I love Whitney's version). Joy to the World even! And of course Teddy Pendergrass, Anita

Baker, Issac Hayes and many others ….recorded songs about this Joy. It is the same Joy God promised His children. That is what I desperately seek. And it is why I continue to write after almost 40 years of up and down experiences called Life. That is why I chose writing and transformative speaking as my retirement life goal.

By God's Grace -- Surviving Life Between a Rock and a Very Hard Place is about my journey. And my testimony shared is without a doubt….. about surviving only by the grace of God.

# Before My Feet Hit the Floor!

Before my feet hit the floor, l want to say THANK YOU. God. I want to praise you for my life, for health, for opening each and every door.

I thank you, Jesus, for family and friends, For the good times as well as the bad

The lessons that everyday living brings.

I pray for our leaders, our children, and anyone in need....I pray for those addicted, afflicted, conflicted, and those consumed with greed.

If I left any one out, Lord - throughout this day, I'll pray some more

I just needed to say

GOOD MORNING and THANK YOU.....

as friends say they do.....

Before my feet.....

HIT THE FLOOR.

I love you God.

Each day I want to praise you

More and more.

# Desperately Seeking

I'm desperately seeking – seeking answers

To the questions nobody's wanting to ask

I'm desperately seeking ways to get rid of

my own disguises and masks! ….I'm desperately seeking.

Desperately seeking peace when the world wants war, desperately seeking

contentment, joy and to be with you God wherever you are!

Praying with the sick, helping those in need, planting hope,

following your lead. I'm desperately seeking. Desperately seeking time.

Right decisions. Rhythm. Rhyme.

Seeking sisterhood from the sisterhood that

Refuses to be a sisterhood,

Seeking dialogue with brothers from Ivory

Towers and brothers from the

hood…..Seeking input on why there are

so many mothers who will never really

know true motherhood. Desperately

seeking – desperately seeking an

awakening from nightmares that haunt me

night and day Desperately Seeking the

Lord and communications with the Holy

Spirit… so He will show me the way! I'm

Desperately Seeking! I'm seeking a

partnership with mankind— a

Memorandum of Understanding.

Direction for the stage play of my life

and these many roles I have landed. I'm

Desperately Seeking.

Desperately Seeking Love/Peace/Hope/Vision/

Financial Freedom and Freedom from

"racist" hiring and thinking, Seeking interactions with a generation

skilled at critical thinking.

I feel so helpless as it appears the whole world is sinking... I'm Desperate,

Desperate. Desperately seeking the person God would have me be...

This isn't B.S. I'm D.S. Desperately seeking! That's me!!!

That poem was written years ago. Today, I continue to desperately seek more time with the Father and more direction from the Holy Spirit. Jesus has already "worked it out." Yes, I struggled many times in the past for this or that. For acceptance. For me to understand others and for others to understand me. Today, God says, stop the worrying and trust and obey! Worry about nothing, Pray about everything. And then God spoke to me. This helps....

# But God Said...

I started to worry this morning about something my boss said to me,

But God said, "Don't worry," that's what God said to me.

I was getting a little down, cause friends and loved ones shunned me,

But with gentleness and compassion, God said, "Don't worry."

That's what God said to me.

My bills were getting behind, I was dodging collectors left and right. But

God said, "Don't worry," when I said my prayers last night.

I thought my buddies were genuine, They'd said they had my back,

But God said don't worry when I learned

They were talking behind my back.

The doctor's report I wasn't ready for, but he

Had to give me the news,

"Don't worry, God said again,

"This battle we won't lose."

The morning news is depressing –food and gas prices are up...
And the stock market is down...

But God tells me don't worry – there is a Higher Ground.

I started to worry this morning about wars around the world.

But God just said to me, "Don't worry" Sister-Girl. So I don't need

to worry anymore about people or their ways,

I know with all my issues, the Holy Spirit always makes a way.

I've much more peace today knowing He meets my every need,

"Don't worry," He says to me – when I get down on my knees.

If you are lost, if you're in despair, "Don't Worry" is my advice.

Talk to God every chance you get – and watch Him change your life.

# For God So Loved the World

For God so loved the world – He gave His Son to us –
Is there anyone or
anything that you love that much?
Who among us today would die
to save the entire world?
Who would bear a heavy cross to save a strange boy or unborn little

girl? If God asked you to do what Jesus did for us…
Would you say "Yes?" Or would you
cry, make excuses, complain, or fuss?
"I can't," "I wish I could" or "God, are you sure I'm the one?"
"Let me get back with you with a referral, cause ……
I know someone – my partner, he's the one!"
What would you say if God spoke to you today?
"Prove your love, don't just say it when you pray."
For God so loved the world – Who or what do we love that much?
That we'd sacrifice our lives – As God and His Son sacrificed for us.

*Thought: Jesus paid the price when He died on Calvary – How much CHANGE do we owe Him – for giving His Life for you and me?*

## Does He Love You? A Valentine's Love

No wrapped gifts, no flowers, no chocolates,

No rings, no cards, no diamond bracelets,

No rubies, no pearls, no earrings, no dinner dates,

No phone calls, no exotic trips,

No stuffed animals, no surprise freights.

Does He Love You?

Does He Not?

Does He Love You?

As You Love Him?

Do You Love Him?

As He Loves You?

No wrapped gifts, no flowers, no chocolates,

No rings, no cards, no diamond bracelets,

No rubies, no pearls, no earrings,

no wristwatches, no dinner dates,

No phone calls, no exotic trips,

No stuffed animals, no surprise freights.

Indeed, He loves you! Yes, He cares,

He's always loved you. He's always there.

He's God and He gives you everything,

Do you take Him for granted when You hear the birds sing?

Do you love Him as He loves you?

He is the one that provides for you!

He is the one who unconditionally loves you!

When you think of Him – Let your light shine, And respond when He asks: Will You Be Mine!

# I Saw Jesus Today

I saw Jesus today,

Hi! How are you, I heard him ask,

I didn't respond – I didn't know that Jesus I would one day ignore.

I saw Jesus today,

He was awfully poorly dressed,

But I didn't greet Him or offer him help… I was too busy taking care of myself.

I saw Jesus today – crippled and begging for food, But I didn't recognize his face,

So I didn't do what a Christian should.

I saw Jesus today being lied on and talked about,

But I didn't know it was Him, so I never opened by mouth. I saw Jesus today in the face of a homeless man,

I didn't know it was Him- I didn't offer my help, In fact, I turned and ran.

I saw Jesus today,

They cut off the lights in His home, If I had known it was Him,

I'd have paid to turn them back on.

Was that Jesus in the face of that woman Who didn't have a penny to her name?

I didn't offer her a cent,

If that was Jesus, yes, I'm ashamed.

Now that I've seen Jesus in the faces of people I've met, I don't hesitate to speak, or offer food, drink, or help. I'm not so quick to judge, and slower to anger too, One never knows when it's Jesus

Who's reaching out to you.

# When You Don't Put God First

Things went from bad to worse,

When I stopped putting God first.

When I stopped praying and

Started playing "sick"

When it was time for church…

Playing dumb when it was time

For doing. Playing

hide and seek When

was time to Seek

The Kingdom of God.

Things got bad, and then they got worse

When I stopped putting

God First.

First the car broke down

Then the rent went up,

Never before had I felt so stuck…

The bills multiplied,

Loans were rejected,

When I stopped putting God first

My entire life was hectic.

Deadlines were missed,

Friends were few,

Of course I pray this never happens to you.

Keep God in your life

Let Him always be first…

It'll happen to you as it happened to me

Everything in your life

Will go from bad to worse..

# I Thank God

When I wake up early in the morning, I thank God….

For everything….

For life and health, peace and love,

I thank Him for the bad, the good.

For sending His Son from up above.

 When I see the noon day sun

Shining down so brightly...

I thank God,

For everything.

For strength, for life, for day, for night,

For family and friends,

All the joy His love brings.

But of all that God does for me

Across the land, across the sea,

I thank Him mostly for molding me

And making me the person He would have me be.

# Blessings Assured

*Somebody was trying to block my blessings.*

But God said, "What I have for you is for you."

You'll be able to accomplish what others won't ever do...

You are MY child,

I am YOUR Assurance Policy, Don't worry about people,

pride, material goods or property.

You don't know the plans I have for you... The steps you take have been ordered for you.

No one can block your blessings no matter what they do...

Keep your eyes on the prize and your mind stayed on me

You will get what is yours - just wait and see. This joy I have – someone tried to take it away, But God said they can't –

not tomorrow, not today.

What can man do – that I haven't already done for you?

Smile when friends talk behind your back...

Keep praying when you feel you're alone in this place,

When Satan comes around tell him to get out of your face.

This joy I have no one can take it from me...

God said I'm His child. If I believe, soon I will see. Do unto others as I would have them do unto me? Umph! I had always thought I'd better do to them before they got a chance to do anything to me...

I had been hurt, abandoned, lied on, mistreated, broken-hearted and stepped on much more than was needed.

But God said turn the other cheek everything will be fine. I'll fight your battles – read it for yourself – vengeance is mine.

So what can I say in the course of the day? When in the fray, trouble comes from this and that way – When folk are trying to block my blessings, steal my joy – pull me down, and talk behind my back...

What can I say other than what God told me: I am HIS Child...He's my Blessed Assurance Policy!

Thought: Blessed Assurance – Jesus is Mine. Oh, what a fortress, Glory Divine.

(Christian Hymn, Fanny Crosby, Hebrews 3:14)

The Bible says: You are the light of the world. A city on a hill cannot be hidden. Neither do people light a lamp and put it under a bowl. Instead, they put it on a stand and it gives light to everyone in the house. In the same way, let your light shine before men that they may see your good deeds and praise your Father in heaven. Matthew 5:16.

# This Tiny Little Light

This tiny light of mine – it's still going to shine

How dare you try to snuff out this light,

Now you know that just isn't right.

Yes, your words are cold and cruel

Your looks cut through me

But my light is still going to shine—

Yes try as you might you can't put it out,

Because this light – you didn't give to me.

Talking behind my back?

Not saying two words to me?

This little light will still shine,

This is God's light – can't you see!

Inside, you must be the one hurting

So on others you inflict your pain,

Where is your little light?

I wonder if ever it will shine again.

My light has to shine

God gave it to me…

There are so many in the darkness

With hearts blinded by hate – eyes that Refuse to see.

Try if you will to put my little light out,

With your attitude of arrogance and the

Way you move about..

But this tiny little light of mine

This tiny little light – yes, it's still going to shine.

Try if you will to put this little light out

Try with all your might… but this tiny little light.

Was ignited with love, faith and hope - not doubt!

This light was made to shine and shine,

This tiny little light of mine,

This is God's light this tiny little light…

This tiny little light of mine!

# Survival Skills

First, seek ye first the Kingdom of God. Yes, I have to remind myself of this….Putting God before man is so very, very important. That is the only way that any of us can have peace. Recently, I was reading Jesus Calling. Without infringing on Sarah Young's copyright, I will share the essence of what was written for the May 11 entry when she wrote that we should personally thank God for our problems.

Young wrote that we should really be thankful we have a loving God that we can take our problems to. When we focus on Jesus, our problems will fade in significance and lose power. The power that problems have on us is that we worry. We get anxious. We are fearful. But Sarah Young writes that many of the situations that we "get caught up" in only entangle our minds and they really are not today's concern. What we have done is borrowed these concerns from tomorrow. So we really have to seek ye first Jesus, our Father and in the place of our worries, He will give us Peace – this peace, she says, flows from God's Presence.

We have all heard the saying "Don't worry about what happened yesterday or what might happen tomorrow." Focus on today – it is a gift that is why we call it the present. And Paul tells us in Philippians 4:6: Do not be anxious about anything, but in every situation, by prayer and petition, with Thanksgiving, present your requests to God.

Another daily devotion: This trouble you're in isn't punishment; it's training, the normal experience of children… God is doing what is best for us, training us to live God's holy best (Hebrews 12:8, The Message). So it is clear we need not focus on our problems or situations and circumstances that seem to be meant to steal our joy. I hope to try to remember this one when I do feel "down and out." Rather than ask God to change our circumstances, ask Him to use our circumstances to change us! This had to be shared in bold print. This is not a message meant just for me.

With that said, you can feel my pain in some of the following poems. Quite often we go through difficulties, but God brings us through them some times just so we can be a blessing to others. That is how the poetry I've written has worked in the past. As personal as it is… usually someone else finds joy, finds peace, finds answers in how to survive life…. When between a rock and a very hard place. God prepares us so when we encounter others who are going through hard times that we can be there for them just like God is and has been there for us. What we go through many times just prepares us for what might happen to us or someone we love in the future. Corinthians 1:3 says "Praise be to the God and Father of our Lord Jesus Christ, the Father of compassion and the God of all comfort, who comforts us in all our troubles, so that we can comfort those in any trouble with the comfort we ourselves receive from God." Praise God!

We can always count on God to use any mess we are in for something good. He says so in Romans 8:28: All things –not some things – but ALL things work together for good to those that love God, and for those who are called according to His purpose. We don't know the plans God has for us. But His plans are to prosper us. His plans are to give us hope and a future. We don't know these plans. Only God knows. He says in Jeremiah 29:11: I know the plans I have for you! We simply need to have continued faith. He keeps His promises.

But even in those times of distress, or worry, or anxiety (all of which we should not have), we also must come into agreement with what Paul says in Philippians 3:7-11 (NIV):

But whatever were gains to me I now consider loss for the sake of Christ. What is more, I consider everything a loss because of the surpassing worth of knowing Christ Jesus my Lord, for whose sake I have lost all things. I consider them garbage, that I may gain Christ and be found in him, not having a righteousness of my own that comes from the law, but that which is through faith in Christ—the righteousness that comes from God on the basis of faith. I want to know Christ—yes, to know the power of his resurrection and participation in his sufferings, becoming like him in his death, and so, somehow, attaining to the resurrection from the dead.

1 Peter 4:12-13 says the same: Beloved do not be surprised at the fiery trial when it comes upon you to test you, as though something strange were happening to you. But rejoice insofar as you share Christ's sufferings, that you may also rejoice and be glad when his glory is revealed. In the world, it is a fact: We will have tribulation (John 16:33). We will have pain. We will have heartbreak. We will have disappointments. I do believe I have had my share, but I also know that God will not put any more on me than I can bear. This book is sincerely my testimony. I know that I have been challenged by the enemy. I know that I have not responded always as Christ would have responded. Now that I know.... I have on the full armor of God to protect me, to protect my heart, and to give me the desires of my heart. The poetry that follows is reflective of those times when writing served as my therapy....those times and situations that forced me to my prayer room!

# IN SURVIVING LIFE: LOVE ON LIFE SUPPORT

# Watching Love Die!

It happened too quickly for me.
In the blink of an eye you see…
One minute we were all over one another
We had promised a lifetime of being one another's lover…

But in the blink of an eye….
We stood there helpless just watching
That precious one –in – a million, always and forever…love die.
At some point we gave it CPR Operated on it, prayed over it,
We even wished for its revival under a falling star. We still
don't know what happened
But here we are. . . .
Trying to keep this love alive,

That's where we are.
Trying to do CPR.
Dialing 911
And praying for miracles
And a Lazarus-breath resuscitation.
Who would have thought?
What we had that was once so alive Is definitely now near death!
Two healers in the house
Watching love die--

Helpless and hopeless. Too late -Not about to resuscitate

Not calling 911. Not requesting an autopsy cause we both know why!

Negligence on both our parts. Because we both sat here and watched our love die.

# I Am Not Your Enemy

Why do you shoot me down with selfishness?
Why are you stabbing me with control?
I am your partner for life
The one you promised to have and to hold.
Why do you hit me with coldness?
And must you always aim for my heart?
Have you forgotten the vows we made?
We both promised love till death do we part.
Why do you slap me with dishonesty,
Why do you choke me with words that hurt?
I am not your enemy, my love.
As a Child of God, this pain I don't deserve.
I am not your enemy
But I am dodging grenades left and right.
Yes, I am fighting back,
I wear the full Armor of God - day and night.
I wear the breastplate of righteousness,
I am protected by the Sword of the Spirit
that is where I find truth.
I am not your enemy.
The Armor I wear .. you should be wearing too.
Where is your helmet of salvation?
Christ died that we might live!
Where is your shield of faith?

I don't know about you, but to Satan,

I have nothing to give.

The vows we took made us one –

One with each other and one with God.

I am not giving Satan anything,

Not my home, not my marriage, not my peace,

I am not giving him my joy, my children...or my hope.

None of this will he take from me. I am not your enemy....

If you think I am your enemy, you are greatly deceived.

Put on your armor now ... let's fight this battle together,

Through prayer and petition, and God leading our way.

It is only id we pray together

That till death do we part.

I am not your enemy.

Satan, please, just let us be.

# If You Can, I Can, and Will

If you can stop accusing, I can stop defending

Myself for crimes I didn't commit.

Like going out every night,

Or staying out ALL night,

If you can stop accusing me of not loving you

I can be more at ease when it comes to giving all my love to you. If

you can stop believing that I am in some calculated

Fight against you, you will see that I am on your side.

That I want what you want and we could easily put our

Weapons aside. For if there was ever a fight it has

Been a fight for you – not against you.

I am not against you or anything, or anyone you love....I am for us.

And if there is anything or anyone who cannot be for us, then I, like you, wish to fight that fight.

I can. And I will.

# But I Stayed Anyway

I smelled cologne on your coat

I heard your whispered calls

I saw the evidence everywhere....

The first signs of the writing on the wall...

I read the notes sent to you

I saw the texts that you sent back

More and more, time and again

The writing was clear on the wall....

The "ex" was trying to get you back.

That's what they do with a "good catch" like you

Yes, they'll use every trick in the book

Now that you are happy and have moved on

They want you to give them a second look

But I am yours and you are mine

Every day I just have to

pray.... Things looked pretty

bad.... but I stayed anyway.

I stayed because I love you

I stayed because God said so

And I feel very strong it is past time

To let you know.

You needed me I needed you

We are in this together for life

Otherwise, it wouldn't have happened

That we would be man and wife.

You are my love

I'd have it no other way..... So tell others to move on

Move out of the way –

This love we have is an enduring love –

Our love is here to stay.

# I Can't Change You

I can't change you - yes, I've been trying to
Trying to make you love me
Trying to make you see me
Trying to make you see how much
I am here for you but I can't change you.
Not sure what you see when you
Look at me - I feel like you're really
Looking through me but you're seeing
The pain of the one who came before me.
The one you couldn't trust.
The one who didn't love you.
The one who didn't respect you.
The one who never saw you
For who you are
The Child of God that you are
That is who I see when I look At you.
Which is also the reason I cannot change you.
Only God can.
Only God will.
Only Time will.
Not me.
I cannot change you.
I can only pray for you.
And I do.

Because I love you.

And want only the best for you.

Lord, protect him.

Guide him.

Comfort him.

Teach him.

Strengthen

him.

Lift him up!

Instill in him

That he can never give up. how him love.

Show him peace.

Show him kindness.

Show him joy.

Show him that

He is a child of the King.

No I cannot change you.

Lord, help me -

Because every day from now on...

I am going to pray for you.

God will work with you,

Just as He works with me

Just so I can love you.

Thanking God I finally listened

And I finally learned.

No matter what I think I can do

I cannot change you!

# Over and Over

I'll say it over and over,

It's one of the perks – that love for one another

I'll say it 24-7, softly in your ear but sometimes

Loudly enough for the whole universe to hear…

I'll say it over and over

I'll say it when you're close by and

I'll say it when you're nowhere near,

When I know you're out chasing moose or deer,

When snow is falling,

When the geese are calling,

When folks are sleeping,

Or dancing in the streets of Memphis or New Orleans,

When it's 110 degrees – I'll say it…

For no reason at all

Or maybe I'll say it just to put your mind at ease.

I'll say it over and over.

It's one of the perks – that love for one another…

I'll say it online,

I'll say it on the phone,

I'll say it in my car,

I'll say it anytime..

And I'll say it over and over…

And over and over and over again….

I'll say it till you hear me loud and clear –

You might even say –

"You don't have to say it anymore,

I got it now, dear."

But until then I'll just keep saying it

Over and over…

What am I saying that you haven't heard today?

What you know in your heart but I will say anyway?

Simply this Love of my life… …

I love you,

I love you,

I love you,

I love you,

I love you

It's one of

the perks

That love

for one

another.

# GOD AND ONLY GOD CAN CHANGE OUR SITUATIONS

## Jeremiah 29:11

# Memories of You

It keeps happening again and again,
I think you're gone... out of my life
The furthest thing from my mind.
Then it happens - in the middle of the night
In the noon day sun, whether I'm bored to death or out having fun.
It hits me -
Memories of you...
The things you and I used to do,
The love we made, the games we played
The dancing, romancing, the taken chances,
All come back out of the blue.
Like now – ahhh the memories of you.
It keeps happening over and over,
And all the while I thought it was over.
I "gave up the ship" some time ago,
But the memories of you – I just can't let them go.

# You Touched Me

You touched me
And my heart skipped
Not just one beat
But nine or ten
There was nothing
Physical
Yet you touched me
With your kindness,
Tenderness,
Your gentle-MAN-ness
You touched me
And I immediately
Became your friend
My heart skipped
 Not just one beat
But one beat
But nine or ten
Can't wait to have you
Touch me again!!

# Me tocaste!

By Juan Bradley (in memory of real friendship)

*Me tocaste y este Corazon de mio, refozo*
*no mas uno palpitacion*
*pero nueve o diez*
*habia nada fisico*
*sin embargo, me tocaste*
*con tu bondad ternura*
*tu hombradia junto con*
*Amabilidad*
*Me tocaste*
*Y yo directamente llega a ser amiga a te*
*Mi Corazon refozo, no mas uno*
*Palpitacion pero nueve o diez*
*No esperar hasta que me tocar*
*Otra vez!!!*

# Open Book

I am an open book Don't look….

- we

- are

- not

- on

- the

- same

Page …

Time someone read me

My right

To remain silent.

I don't however.

I sometimes talk loud and

Say nothing

That anyone wants to really hear.

Hear ye hear ye, the court of love

Is not quite back in session..

# Expecting A Breakthrough

I have been expecting way too much
Thinking the waters will break
And somehow ease the heartache
The labor pains me when I expect
So much of you....
Trying every day to please you
Spend time with you
Assist you
Do my very best for you
While expecting you might
Do the same for me.
But that is too much
I can finally see I need
Not wait for you to
Love me.
I need not wait for you
To wine and dine me.
I need not wait.
This isn't a baby
This is Marital Reality.
I am expecting a breakthrough
 Before I experience a breakdown
I am waiting for the waters to
Break - thinking love will abound.

But that is my fantasy,

My foolishness,

My silly ass dream,

Expecting you to be somebody

You have never been.

Expecting, Expecting.

Waiting and waiting.

The labor pains me

I need an epidural,

Or maybe just a breakthrough….

Or a break-out…

Damn sure not planning

To live my life unloved….

That just leads to a Breakdown.

Help me God! I know…

*You are my real Breakthrough*!


*Life isn't perfect. People are not perfect. Sometimes not so pretty thoughts enter the mind. Over time you become emotionally drained fighting for what you think you want and what you know to be right. But in the end and at all times you have to determine the armor you will wear and the shield you keep near.*

# Not Anymore

I don't want to be around you
Any more than you
Might dare possibly "want" to be
Around me.
We operate as if we are
Two passing ships in
The night
No light house
No light at all…..
We collide
Even in broad daylight
Two passing ships
Every day
Every night.

# A Love Revelation

I loved you much more than I loved myself…

Otherwise, I wouldn't have allowed you to put me on the shelf.
I wouldn't have been "saved for a rainy day," cast aside or tossed away.
If I had loved me
As much as I loved you,
The things you did to me
Would have been done back to you.
But I was too much in love,
To ever do you wrong,
And with every insult you gave me
I just went right along,
Loving you and loving you
More than I could ever love me,
Thank God I've now learned to love me,
Which is really the way
God intended for it to be.

# Love

Love is a figment of one's imagination
A hint or obvious indication
A thought, a little consideration
Love is a quiet infatuation.
Genuine Love – a Key
 Ingredient for Survival

# Never Yes and Never No!

He loves me?

He loves me not!

Does it really matter?

He gives it his best shot.

Were it not for the question, never being answered…

I certainly would never have known the difference.

But question was always asked,

The answer never yes nor was it no….

You know the facts as well as I. …… What's that?

Love is not what you say but what you show.

# You'll Wish I Still Cared

You're going to wish that I still cared

Like the times when I cared about the fact

That you wouldn't call me when you said you would.

Yeah, you're going to wish that I still cared.

And what about all those trips that you had to take by yourself, to be
in your space and get in touch with yourself…ot telling me where you
were going or when you might return

Seeing you just disappear without a care or concern! It was definitely
inconsiderate, and yes unfair, but one day, just wait, you'll wish I still
cared. Evidently, I was a nuisance

When unconditionally I cared,

Like when I'd ask:

"When will you be back, Baby just tell me!"

"Don't you want me to go? "Don't you want my company?" Just my
way of caring – just me being me,

Hungry for you and your love and your time,

But that was when you were always on my mind

That was when I cared and wanted to be with

You all the time. Believe me, one

day you'll wish I still cared likethat

One day you'll wish you had me back,

One day you'll wish I still cared, but today I don't.

You think I'll let the chips fall where they may

But I won't. Maybe you don't know what it means to care, Maybe you don't know true love when it's in the air. Maybe one day you'll realize that you needed me there. I guarantee you'll wish one day I still cared…. One day you'll wish that I would call you on the phone…and come hang out with YOU, so you won't be alone,

You'll remember how I was there for you…

guess you just didn't know how much I cared for you. It's gonna happen- keep ignoring me if you dare –Trust me. One day you'll wish that I still cared.

# Loving You To Death

I can only love you with half my heart
The whole is too much for you.
You say I'm being emotional,
That I might agree to too.
But I called it love,
I called it caring.
I called it simply
Loving you to death –
And maybe that was the problem
When you needed space and time for self.
I called it togetherness, oneness,
A unified love.
It was simply
A pleasure for me
When you were all I could think of.
I called it Seventh Heaven,
Heaven on Earth,
And forever on Cloud Nine.
While I hoped you loved me
With all your heart,
I knew I loved you with all of mine.
And maybe that was the problem,
When you needed space and time.

So with only half my heart
I shall love you.
Giving you space, time and whatever else you need, my friend, my
love,
So that I don't in fact
Love you to Death.

# Loved Redefined

It was not about feeling great
Or "Extremely Excited" anymore.
And it hardly had anything to do
With fantasies, romance, what was
Fashionable or Fictional.
Rather it was all about being
Close, safe, and secure.
Comfortable, satisfied, and
Completely in control.
It was about a rare pleasure
A special joy in sharing my life
With you.
It was what some call love—
And what I call LIFE… meant to be.l

## Nonsense

I kept thinking
And thinking
Of you….
And wondering just what
I'd do
If you were ever to
Go away
And stay
And say
You didn't love me
The way
You used to…Just
The thought of that
Sets me back
A lifetime you know.
So please just tell me
It's nonsense

# My Kind of Love

IIt wasn't really love at first sight,

Cause neither of us were swept off our feet.

But there was enough interest

To investigate the possibility of compatibility.

It lasted long enough to say it was good.

It was short enough that if necessary

It could be forgotten with time.

It really was my kind of love.

The kind of love that doesn't hurt...

Too much.

# How Else?

I had to hear it
Feel it
Speak it
To know it
And show it
I had to live it
See it… I had to.
To believe it.
I had to.
How else
Would my heart
Go on beating
Wondering….
If you loved me
The way I love you.
I really had to know
If you loved me or not.
Keeping It Light, Keeping It Real
…with God's Grace Still Surviving!
A little recovery haiku….

# Haiku-ing!

## Reminiscing

Reflecting is almost the same
As reminiscing. It is
Drawing on past thoughts.
It is an art form
Using colors, pencils,
ink,
Brushes, paint and sidewalk chalk.
Erratically splashed joy and pain -
Mental canvases come to life
The art perfected.

## Breaking News

Two speak again
Man busted for
Innocent lies
To daughter and wife.
Fight Resolved Psycho
Logical breakthrough.
Don't fix things
That don't fix you.

## Missing

When I found
My missing
Cross
I heard God say all
was Not lost.

## Blessing

Four a.m. alarm
from God.
Message: Sleeping
again through your
blessing.

## Philippians 4:13

Doing all things
Through Christ
Strengthens me
Verse restores my Sanity.

## Insight

Discernment. Father,
This gift, yes, 'Dis discernment
Can be disturbing.

## Cussing

So mad fit to be
Tied so tired of lies yes I'm
Fussing and cussing.

## Fishing

He and I like to fish
He catches steelhead trout
I fish for answers.

# Laughing

I keep laughing at you
And the foolish things you do
How you try to make a fool of me
Not knowing that God is protecting me.
So I keep laughing …
At you
Your selfish ways
Your mean spirit
Your nasty attitude
So I send up a prayer
When you're so unfair
And I keep laughing and
Laughing at you.
Forgive Him father
He knows not the likes of you.
Satan has him all tied up
He doesn't know the left from the right
He tries his best to pull me down

So I laugh – instead of crying at night.
I can't help it .
I keep laughing at you,
Making a fool of yourself,

When you wanted to make a fool
Out of me.
But can't with God and the Angels
Watching me....
Yes, they are laughing too
They're laughing right along with me.

# A Few Too Many No's.....

No I won't pray with you
Do yoga with you/go dancing/or listen to
jazz around the corner or the next town over or play cards tennis
or chess with you.
I won't plan vacations or travel with you
I won't pay the bills I promised to pay
I have no intentions of delivering on what I say…Stop asking
because no I am not buying
Clothes or shoes or cars for you…..
I won't give you access to my accounts
Or passwords to hotel points or discounts.
No I won't be going to church with you,
Or counseling either and no
I want take those silly nature walks
with you.
Don't recommend any movies- that's out too.
My mind is made up
Before you ask –
Every answer will be: No to you!!

## With Tenderness, I Think of You

When I think of you, it is unquestionably with tenderness. For that
is you - the way you love and show love.

It is always with tenderness, Unquestionably. Thus, therefore, and
forevermore –

When I think of you…..

Your Tenderness, Love, and Gentleness

Emanate….. through and through.

# One Con Too Many

I am convinced, you are confused, the contest is contested, the

contract discontinued. The convenience has been convoluted

and is hereby disconnected.

There is absolutely no contempt considered or construed.

The contentment is on.

When I am convinced that one is confused,

I concede that the conquest was counterfeit.

Let's consider the experience – just one con too many.

# SOCIAL CONSCIOUSNESS

Being "woke" in the 21st Century is a Survival Requirement

# The Color Line Revisited: is "Ray" Cism Dead?

"Ray" Cism is old and not yet dead, how could "Ray" Cism die -- if he's in your heart, your mind, or your head? When was the last time you went to church with someone who didn't look like you?

What color were their eyes? Green, grey, brown, black or blue? If Ray Cism is dead, just how did he die? Were you in on his demise or did you stand off to the side? Perhaps you turned your head when others were the target - just thankful it wasn't you – so you didn't bother to stop it. Ray Cism is bold where redistricting is concerned, and no one's quite forgotten Black churches that were burned. Does your pizza man deliver – not afraid to drive down your street? Or are you zoned way too Black – and drivers are afraid they might get beaten? When you went to Denny's, Cracker Barrel, and Waffle House, were you greeted with a smile? Or were you turned away - disappointed because the servers' attitudes were foul? No – bias doesn't flow in one narrow (minded) direction. Look at LGBT individuals who have been assaulted, their pain, their rejection. Everyone's been a victim at one time or another.

The Japanese were interned and Jews in Germany were gassed and smothered. But America is the Land of the Free, the home of the Brave. There's no room for cowardice; that's no way to behave. "Ray" Cism/ Racism is certainly not yet dead, but I pray it will soon go away. It can, it will if we each respect one another – and let God lead our way.

# Pressed

Black people have always
Been pressed.
We've been oppressed,
Depressed,
And just pressed –
For time,
For love,
For jobs,
For money…
For somebody to take
The chains off us.
Black people have been
Suppressed to no end,
So pressed we don't ever seem to win,
Much of anything.
Black people have always been pressed.
But in spite of it all – Black people !!
We are blessed.
We are blessed.

.

# Still, You Rise

He stole you away from Africa – And made you work "his" land,

He beat you down like an animal – the pain you were made to

withstand.

You persevered, you've "overcome," you've done more than "survive."
You are businessmen, you are family

Providers, in spite of it all you Rise!

The Middle Passage was very rough, thousands died along the way,
Stacked, packed, viciously attacked – yes the pain we feel today.

But the ancestors maintained, in God our Strength lies….it's 2020
Brothers and Sisters, And yes.. Still you rise

Unemployment is out of hand, Downsizing is here to stay.

The political front is frightening, And certainly gives us reason to pray.

But you my brothers and sisters have survived so much: Equal rights

and other lies…..

Keep pushing, keep praying, keep standing tall!

With God, you'll always rise!!!!!

# The Revolution Is Not Over

TThe revolution is not over

The fires have not gone out.

The posters are 30 years faded,

"Burn. Whitey, Burn," T

he voices now whisper,

Once so strong, they used to shout!

But the revolution is not over.

Equal rights, affirmative action are soon a

Thing of the past,

The playing fields are said to be equal –

But how long will this last?

The revolution is not over.

African-American Negro Black People…

Driving MercedesVolvosLexusRolls

African-American-Negro-Black people

Too busy to get to the polls.

The playing fields are said to be equal

The coach and quarterback are Black.

They gave us the Civil Rights

Bill And now they are taking it back.

The Revolution is not over

Black churches being burned,

Black men still going to jail,

Serving twice the time,

Paying twice the bail.

The Revolution best not be over.

Black women being uppity!!

# Yo '/Your Child Left Behind

When President Bush finishes with us, the speech, the act, the theme –
No Child Left Behind will be in reality

Yo' Child Left Behind.

Left behind in Iraq – as we commence our attack

Behind in Afghanistan, Pakistan, you-do-understand??

Our volunteer armed services signed on when the

Unemployment ran out….Some with degrees

Spent time on their knees

Praying but the checks stopped coming – And now there is talk of

A Draft?? Rangel suggested it to get people

To start thinking but no amount of thinking in the world can stop

evil when evil is determined to rule…

Slogans are cute. Sound bytes are sweet.

But something has to be done

When Americans are sleeping on the street.

No Child Left Behind?

Listen closely and look at the writing on the wall…

You're sleeping again through God's wake up call…

Isn't it Yo' Child Left Behind,

Behind the corporate run prison walls,

Behind in our colleges because of lack of funding,

Behind in basically everything…

These are the blues I'll always sing…

As I look at the schools in my neighborhood…

As I look at the Capitol Hill's Robin Hoods…

It isn't No Child Left Behind…

It's clear as day –

It's yo' child …. You'll see who's left behind.

# It's Just a Little Word –
# The Little Word Up!

It's just a little word, That little word "up."
Think of starting your day – you've first got to wake up.
Don't hit the snooze button. Brothers and Sisters Get up!
And if you do as the ancestors instructed,
A prayer or two you immediately send up.
After you have showered and freshened up,
You think of what you'll wear, and maybe –
Maybe you'll dress up.
You look at the clock and realize you better speed up.
So you hurry up and eat breakfast and pray
On Cold mornings the vehicle will start up.
You pick up some energy when you see the sun has come up,
And you get stirred up when you reflect on the
Opportunities out there for you to move up.

There's no doubt in your heart it will happen
Because Grandma, the church, Pastors' wife
And even the Mother Board and the Choir
have lifted your name up. You dread admitting
it but you know that on that job
You sometimes have to kiss up.
What you don't want to do is something
Stupid and mess up.
You leave early enough in the morning
so in traffic you are not held up.

Certainly, when things don't unfold as planned,
You dare not give up. And the last thing you want is to know that
Your time is up not once in your life did you stand up and speak up.
You can't keep up with the Joneses if your
Retirement you spend up;
And please don't try to sweep up
around someone else's doorway
if you haven't kept up your own yard.
FIX UP yourself.
With knowledge.
FILL up your mind.
You can be assured of moving up if you keep
On looking up and depending on God.
Didn't you know??? He's got the real hook-up.

# John Lewis' Mama Didn't Raise No Fool

At this time in history, we have got to be real. Bill
Clinton was never a Black President and could never
know what a Black person really feels… "John, you owe
me" in Selma of all places Bill said to John. "I promised
Hillary the White House way back in 1971." "She goin'
need your support and your people's vote, too,
I'm telling you John, I'm counting on you.
But John's mama Mrs. Willie Mae Lewis from Troy, Alabama
…. Didn't raise no fool.
John marched with Dr. King in Nashville
When he was a student in school,
Would he turn back a Civil Rights clock that he himself helped set?
Would he be a 21st Century "New Negro,"
Who so easily could forget?
Forget the struggles?
Forget the lunch counters?
Forget the lynching?
Forget the auction counter?

Forget Birmingham?

Forget Rosa Parks?

Forget Emmett Till?

Forget racial profiling after dark?

Forget Shirley Chisholm?

Barbara Jordan, Ron Brown, Mickey Leland, Fannie Lou Hamer???

Harriet Moses Tubman? Forget Martin's Dream

That Obama had made real...

For our youth in 2008????

No!!! John Lewis' mama didn't raise no fool—

John Lewis told us to make good trouble,

His mother definitely didn't raise no fool.

# NFL Political Madness

You mad because they are kneeling,

Exercising freedom of speech...

But you didn't get mad when Nazi's

Were screaming and yelling on Charlotte's streets.

You are NOT mad because of a flag

These professional players are not unpatriotic - that's a fact...No you

are mad because they have courage.     And you're mad because they are

rich.and moreso because they are BLACK!!!

# To The Brothers

To the strong brother who reaches out

And touches the lives of other,

Who isn't afraid of helping sisters,

Or protecting mothers.

The brother who doesn't waste time on games

Collecting numbers and bragging "no shame."

To the caring brother who leads the way

And isn't afraid to speak out,

The brother whose voice is easily heard

Without having to curse or shout.

The brother who doesn't "waste" time at all

Or waits for the next brother or sister to fall.

To the loving brother who is very sincere


And is willing to be loved

Who isn't afraid of opening up

And sharing the stuff he's made of

The brother who doesn't waste energy

Focusing so much on the negativity.

To the brother who can be held close

And is less concerned with being "The Man."

Who listens, trusts, and partners with….

His very special woman.

The brother who doesn't waste a moment

Doing what has to be done.

We love you brothers…..

You are Number One!!!

# Martin, Nelson, Malcolm, Robert, and John

Martin, Nelson, Malcolm, Robert, and John
Dare we go where they have gone?
Martin to the Mountaintop,
Nelson's fight against apartheid – truly nonstop.
Malcolm travelled to Mecca and saw the world
With new eyes.
Returning to America filled with hope and pride.
JFK said, "Ask not what your country can do for you."
But what did we do? Just what did we do?
John went to his grave – ever so brave,
He called for legislation that would one day
Set us free? Abraham couldn't do it?
Dare we ask, could he?

Martin jailed down in Birmingham,
Beaten in Selma,
Stabbed in New York,
Shot down in Memphis,
Cause he had a dream.
Martin, Nelson, Malcolm, Robert, and John,
Dare we go where they have gone.
Walking through the valleys of the Shadow of Death,
Fearing no evil,
Thinking of more than themselves,

Do we dare go where they have gone.

Have we the courage of Nelson to stand up and fight?

When Blacks are the majority,

But ruled by Whites.

Fighting for equality Nelson spent 27 years in jail,

Can any of us follow along Mandela's brave trail?

Malcolm X once had hatred in his heart,

He had seen injustice right from the start,

He issued a call for love and brotherhood,

Only to be assassinated by his own blood.

Robert and John were brothers –

Kennedy's you know.

Shot down in America

Cause they spoke out for the Negro.

Marching through the valleys of the

Shadow of Death,

Pursuing equality for all –

Not just for themselves.

Do we dare go where either of these men have gone?


Front line generals – Martin, Nelson, Malcolm, Robert, and John.

Some men see things as they are, and ask why.

I dream of things that never were, and ask why not.

Where have they all gone –Martin Nelson Malcolm Robert and

John??


*Faith does not make things easy, it makes them possible. Luke 1:37*

# Black Women Marching On and On

Madam C. J. Walker – Sojourner Truth – Nikki Giovanni – and
Gwendolyn Brooks
And the list goes on and on. Of famous Black women who stood
out from the crowd,
Self-confident, informed, Black and Proud,
Who knew who they were as they stood alone,
The strength of these women lives on and on.
Constance Baker Motley – Barbara Jordan – Pauli Murray -
Phylis Wheatley –Maxine Waters,
They came as lawyers and judges and writers,
Abolitionists, educators, determined fighters.
Dreamers of Dreams – PRAY-ers of Prayers,
Each had a dance, each had a song,
They stood for a lot,
At times they stood alone.
Strong Black women moving on.
Jasmine Crockett - Ida Wells Barnett – Susan Taylor – Judith Jamison
– Katanji Jackson– Bessie Coleman, Marching, enduring, burning the
midnight oil,
Living loving, not afraid to toil.

Not afraid to stand even when it meant standing alone,

These Queens from Africa go on and on.

Dorothy Height – Coretta Scott King – Daisy Bates

– Aretha Franklin -Billie Holiday – Ella Fitzgerald -

Patricia Roberts Harris – Myrlie Evers Williams – Mae Jemison –

Nancy Greene, Dianna Ross,

No mountain too high/ No valley too low/ No river too wide/

Nothing stops them

Not anymore. So they march to the beat of a different drummer

And they move with a steady, unending beat…

They take pride in standing tall and strong,

Courageous Black women moving on.

Not taking "no," not accepting defeat.

Ruby Dee – Mary Church Terrell – Edmonia Lewis…. Making this

a better world.

Camille Cosby – Harriett Ross Tubman – Winnie Mandela – Leotyne Price – Fannie Lou Hamer. Oprah Winfrey, Daisy Bates, Katherine Johnson, Nina Simone….and now Kamala Harris….. YES

the list goes on and on.

Underground Railroads/Risking Their Lives/In search of Freedom's Path/Harriet In disguise/Watchful/Witty and So Very Wise.

Shirley Chisholm – Maya Angelou – Angela Davis –

Mary McLeod Bethune,

Queens of Queens, The Exalted Ones. Standing for Justice---

She stands alone. Standing for Peace, for Love, Equality…The list goes on and on.

Mary Frances Berry – Lena Horne – Rosa Parks – Florence Griffith Joyner,

Educators, Legislators, Historians, Leaders, the struggle goes on and on.

The battle is not over, it has barely begun,

She stands tall, The Black Woman, though she doesn't mind standing alone.

The epitome of survival, she stands strong,

Madame C. J. Walker – Sojourner Truth – Nikki Giovanni – Gwendolyn Brooks

Judges and writers, abolitionists, fighters, dreamers of dreams, PRAY-ers of Prayers,

Singing their songs – The list goes on …and on… and on… Black women keep marching on and on.

# KAMALAHARRIS

K eep

A scending

M other/Sister of A frican descent L ead

A merica H elp

A merica R id us of R acism

I t is

S ystemic.

# Just for You

Rosa sat so Ruby could walk,

So Shirley could show possibilities…

So you could run and win….

And courageously you are racing to bring about change.

You are facing doubters, critics, skeptics, naysayers too…

The stubborn, the insecure, the incorrigible, the un-informed of many hues. The ill-advised continue to lie.

Unqualified and loud - the truth they deny.

The underachievers are overreacting - undermining you and creating crises,

….But you must keep running.

Rosa sat so Ruby could walk, so Shirley show possibilities

So you could run and win

and make it to the House, the White House of course!

So you could each this first in our lifetime plateau

So you could gain the support of millions –

People like me, people you might never know!

This is not just any race -

This race is of the people, by the people, for the people in 2024.

This race is not about DEI as some would suggest,

This race is about the Future of America and which leader is best!

Yes there is dog-whistling, name-calling, stereotyping, and gas-lighting,
But we are above that - be assured we're gonna keep on fighting.....

Because Rosa sat so Ruby could walk, so Shirley could show possibilities,
So you could run and win!

And you WON!

You won the hearts and millions.

You won on ethics, intelligence, engagement.

You won.

You won because you taught us:

We are definitely not going back.

# Moving on Up... Or Are We Being Moved Out?

George Jefferson, Weezie and Florence moved on up

I can't recall who it was that was doing the White House

Presiding but I know who's there now

But those of us in the sixties

Unknowingly became sociological projects

Residing in George Washington Carver

 And Harriett Tubman Homes

Are now being moved out by Urban Planning Developers

With high rise conveniences

Lofty ideas and billions of Benjamins

That's more than enough dough to play

Hide and seek with as Big Government friends and your

Very own elected officials hide the master plan

Of buying up all the inner city land.

You already know if you don't have a plan

The slave master surely has a plan for you.

Do you know your councilman, your state

Representative, your state senator and who's in DC?

You waste your right to vote if you don't

Demand accountability.

You might have thought school busing was disruptive

And reasonable cause for cussing.

Just wait until you see brothers and sisters

With NO WAYS AND MEANS of getting into town to

Work that 9 to 5 or that 7 to 3….

If you live downtown, you walk to work or

Catch the trolley – it's free…

Lord have mercy

Cause the buses don't cater to those in the suburbs.

Why should they???

Except to bring the maid and the yard man in?

Mass transit is for the masses not the massa's…. and

Not dreaming the American Dream of home ownership,

Minimum wages, and less than good credit have always

Been enough to keep uneducated, rowdy, unemployed,

Employed and educated not that rowdy Negroes out..

But Negroes were getting college degrees back in the sixties…

From those HBCUs built by the slaves for master's

Children of the darker hue.

And that's when White Flight really reached a new height…

Don't leave it to Beaver to know what's going on.

You got to read the paper to know what's happening

To your promised 40 acres.

"A Negro next door? One is okay but did you say there were more?"
DuBois would be proud of the talented tenth…

The cream he dreamed about that would

One day rise to the top.

The disenfranchised becoming true to life

In his star "Bucks" franchise…

Those with the selected incentives

That achieved a bit more than Booker T's

Labor-intensives in the field harvesting somebody else's crop.

You need to listen closely because his-story, call it history if you want –
Just might be "Your"

Story in the making.

Then came the City Fathers in black and blue suits and silk neckties,
Holding blueprints with small print that would change lives.

They served papers to Negro homeowners and spoke of "Imminent
Domain."

The bottom line: What we had

Worked for and saved for would be the city's gain.

They devalued property with little or no shame.

They wrote small checks and walked away with big plans.

They had their own appraisals,

The deals closed with no if, buts or ands…

Urban Renewal was in

The middle income Negro was out

And it's happening today

As families at all income levels

 Are moved out.

Life-long renters

Aging elders

Section 8 mamas

Project dwellers

Property now selling at 80 to 100K or more a lot.

Revitalizing downtown a national

Trend that is very hot.

Tax break incentives, Attractive loans –

Million-dollar condos –

 The homeless all gone


Where???

Fish isn't frying in the kitchen,

There will be no more front porch grills –

It took George, Weezie, and Florence years

Of trying but they finally got up to Big League Hill!

They started a business and moved on up!

But look closely brothers and sisters, it's 40 years later….

What's gonna happen to the rest of us??

# Connecting the Dots

The key to connecting the dots is green.

The dots are pawn-like chess pieces…

Red and yellow, black and white

Moves first, of course… The haves

Have no baton to hand off.

This is not a race but it is about race.

 And connecting the dots.

The have nots can't wait for a handout.

The key to connecting the dots is green.

Look closely before you take your hand

off

Your p-e-a-c-e (peace) might be in danger…

If you ever had any.

The key to connecting the dots is green

Decision-making haves creating wealth

For themselves…Green the have-nots will never see, decision-making

haves with political clout…

Left-behind have-nots won't even vote them out…

The key to connecting the dots is green…

It is not a game. There is no baton to hand off.

No hand-out to hold up. The dots are red, yellow, black. White….but

the connection is definitely green.

# Talking About You

I'm talking about you

The hater – the One God still loves,

He'll fight my battles

You can't stop what He does.

He has the power to change even you

Don't ever think that He approves of

The things that you do…

He created us – from the angels to the agitators

You just happen to be what some of us call haters…

Blocking the blessings of future generations

Being selfish and cruel, overflowing with mis-education.

I'm talking about you, but I'm leaving it to God,

The one and the Only One able to change your heart!

# Waking Up to Make the Dream a Reality Today

He was not just a dreamer,

He was not just a leader,

He was not just a planner

He was not just a marcher

He was a dreaming, leading,

planning marching man who took a stand

And changed this land.

He was not just a leader

He was not just a preacher

He was not just a mover

He was not just a shaker

He was a leading, preaching, moving, shaking, ground-breaking

Peace-making man… who some would never understand.

He was not just a husband

He was not just a father,

He was not just a son

He was not just a brother

He was Reverend Dr. Martin Luther King

A man determined to hear the bells of Freedom Ring. He tore down the walls of injustice and pain - this broken nation he reached down to Pull u/Pick up,/Build up again and again.

He wasn't just a neighbor

He wasn't just a scholar,

He wasn't just a mentor

He wasn't just a friend.

He was God-sent: This dreaming planning,

Marching, leader, teacher, preacher,

Mover, shaker, husband, father,

Son, brother determined neighbor,

Respected scholar, meticulous

Mentor, faithful friend… This one like

None before. Like none since.

If you didn't know him, learn about him

you didn't meet him, don't think

We didn't need him,

Remember him, celebrate him,

Elevate him, be like him…the King…

The Reverend Dr. Martin Luther King, Jr

Dreaming of a Wake-up Call

And waking us up to Reality…

God-sent like Moses leading a people

Out of a Slave Mentality,

God-sent like Jacob –

What a dream, what a dream.

God-sent like Jesus – He was on

A Mission from the start.

Jailed like Paul and Silas, thrown in the den

Like David.

Loved for his courage.

Loathed because of his power.

Remember him. Celebrate him.

Elevate him. Be like him…

Step out on faith,

Know your purpose.

Put others first.

He trusted and served the same God

You know today.

A God that speaks to you in the very same way.

Dr. King was the Dreamer…

You are the Dream.

Speak up.

Step up.

Get stirred up.

Wise up.

Honestly….

Wake up and make the dream a true reality today.

# In America, It Takes a Village

In America, it takes a village to raise the children we see

The children labeled Generation X, Bebe's Kids, at risk, latchkey...

They are our children, our daughters, our sons, those paying our Social Security

The children in our village are depending on you and me,

It takes a village in America to raise the children we see.

We can begin by monitoring and addressing what they see on TV

Write letters to the Networks – and block out BET, MTV and that unreal,

Reality TV…. And make some noise in DC – demand accountability with the FCC.

Listen to their music – Limit their video games – As you are paying them their

Allowance – pay attention to the children you see.

Why are the children pierced and tattooed, do-ragged and wearing multicolor hair?

Doesn't a dentist care?... Or is it his own bling -bling he sees?

Do your own children need baggy pants, Tommy? FUBU, Coach, designer bags, designer jeans?

Did they inherit their materialistic tastes – is it in your DNA, your genes? Must they drive new cars with rims and the most loaded SUVs?

Did you fail to teach common courtesy like hello, thank you, I'm sorry or please…

How many are leaving home with credit cards and debt?

But have never been taught how to read a cookbook? Balance a checkbook,


Or know how to write a check?

They've got cars but no computers,

Fine clothes but no cash,

They've left the village unprepared,

They've all the answers –

but no questions will they

ask…

They've got guns and game, they've got drugs but little

hope, They're missing out on God, a conscious,

Basic skills, and they don't have a clue about how to cope. In America, it takes a village to raise the children we see,

Write your Homeland legislators and tell them to channel more dollars To Your Village Security.

In America, every villager is at risk – the village has no boundaries We all have duties, we all have responsibilities.

In America, it takes a village,

It takes the elders, the storytellers,

The singers, the writers, anthropologists, psychologists, and meteorologists,

It takes the nurses, the neighbors, the not-so-well known….

The teachers, the lawyers, the surgeons and sanitary workers, electricians and engineers,

It takes the mechanics, machinists, the firefighters, the crime fighters,

The judges, jazz artists, print artists, journeymen, jewelers and journalists. It take

The poets and the plumbers, the politicians and the preachers, the bus drivers

Cab and Metro/Monorail/Amtrak drivers, those who drive nails and those who do nails.

In America, it takes the dreamers, the dentists, the dairy farmers, the Doormen, the DJ, the daycare workers, the social workers, steel workers,


Mine workers, and the plain old Hard Workers. The list could go on and on.

That is the village won't you agree…

And in America it takes the village to raise the children we see.

# Balti…MORE…..or Less

Madam Mayor
Had you given them
Jobs and Rec Centers
Opportunities
Hope ….
Hugs…
Maybe you
Might have seen
They were children
And not called them
Thugs.

# Reporting Black America's Blues

When I re-write
Yesterday's news
I will write on
Trayvon's dreams
Walter Scott's plans
Tamir's future hopes Eric
Garner's passion Michael's
kindness Freddie Gray's goodness.
What I read in yesterday's news
Was the same ole same ole:
When the shooter
Is shot …in the line Of duty
His life is highlighted
And headlined:
The promotions earned
The family left behind
The years served

The potential cut short.
Written against national
ninth hour deadlines.
When unarmed black
people's lives are cut short

Petty crimes are underlined
Headlines of their good are
Overshadowed by broken
Asphalt and bloodstained chalk lines.

# UNDENIABLE DNA

# God Hears and Answers Prayer

My mother taught me years ago
When I was but a child,
To get down on my knees and pray
MORE than just once in awhile.

Now I lay me down to sleep,
I prayed faithfully each night.
I pray the Lord my soul to keep,
Trusting with all my might.
If I should die before I wake,
Would God do that I thought.
And I wondered what that meant.
I pray the Lord my soul to take,
Then I became more content.
Mother made sure my prayers were said.
 But if I somehow forgot –
Out of bed she'd get me,
Skipped prayers she did not allow.
The older I got I came to know
The value of prayer indeed.
I prayed for friends and family, and all
I knew were in need.
It seemed quite clear to me that God heard my prayers –

 As sooner as I said "Amen"

Burdens seemed lighter right then and there.
I prayed for friends who'd lost their faith,
And those who found dead ends.
Loved ones who were hooked on drugs.
And who refused to make amends.
The neighbor whose home had burned down,
The engineer downsized.
 The teen who'd run away from home –
And the parents left traumatized.
Yes, I asked God for faith and strength,
Forgiveness, peace, and love.
I knew He was a loving Father
Who sent many blessings from above.
I knew He listened, I knew He cared,
Mother made this very clear to me,
Ask and you shall receive
There's no one greater than He.
Yes, I still get on my knees
I still call on the God above,
I still hear Mother's gentle voice,
And I feel her unconditional love.
Now I lay me down to sleep
Lord, fill my heart with peace.
Give me understanding
I want to draw nearer to Thee.
God bless my friends and family,
Even those who cause me pain.
Teach me patience, love, and joy,
As I call on you again and again.

And when I am done with life on earth,
I pray you'll take me in.
Giving me a home on high,
I love you, God, my friend.
Yes, I can hear Mother's voice
Telling me always to pray..
You won't get far in life, Child
If you don't let God lead the way.

# That's Where Mother Is

Where a green garden grows,

Where happiness shows,

Where babies are tucked in.

Where floors are scrubbed,

Where everyone's loved,

That's where Mother is.

Where pies are baked,

Where nothing's faked,

Where everyone's invited in,

Where apples are peeled,

Where all wounds are healed,

That's where Mother is.

Where strangers are fed,

 Where kind things are said,

Where losers always win,

Where everyone shares,

Where someone cares,

That's where Mother is.

Where burdens are lightened,

Where dark days are brightened,

Where you know you've got a friend.

Where someone rids you of your fears

And someone wipes away your tears,

You can be sure ... That's where Mother is.

# When Mother Is Gone

You'll think of things

You should have done

Once your mother is gone,

The smallest of small things you did not do –

Will suddenly become should-haves to you....

Once your mother is gone.

The words unspoken, the hugs not hugged,

The visits not made, and the misunderstandings that could have easily been Understood…

Once your mother is gone.

You'll think of the errands you didn't take time to run,

The flowers not sent – the list goes on,

You'll think and think when your mother is gone,

The laughs you didn't take time to laugh,

The praises not praised –

Did you ever think just to rub her shoulders or pat her on the back… You think of these things when mother is gone…

The hands that could have been held a lot more…and times you could have simply swept up the floor! Fixed a door, or filled a prescription,

So many things you could have done,

Now you wonder why you skipped them…

Now that mother is gone.

The times when you could have just sat a spell,

Taken out the garbage or sorted her mail. Called her up, wished her well,

Run her bath or clipped her nails....

Little things you can count

One by one,

But it's too late now - now that mother is gone. For someone - Mother is alive and waiting,

Never complaining, God gave her such patience,

She smiles each time she thinks of you,

Remembering you as a child and the things you used to do.

Every once in awhile, she sheds a tear or two,

Is that your mother alone and blue?

If so, stop and pick up the phone,

Don't let the day come when you're thinking and thinking and thinking And thinking...

Of little things for your mother....

You could have done.

# What God Has For Me –
# A Wise Mother Said

A wise mother once told me something perhaps you've heard before too,
You know mothers always have words of wisdom –

They're more than happy to share with you.

What she said has forever stuck in my mind:

She said, "Child slow down and take life one day at a time."

I had been rushing through my busy life –

an overachiever you might say….

But not having joy or peace at the end of my very busy day.

Not feeing fulfilled at all, and quite often simply feeling a mess.

Trusting my judgment, foolishly thinking I knew

what was best. My judgment with jobs oh I've had plenty,

I'd work a few months then realize they just weren't me.

It was either the people, the pressure, the pay or the pace,

Going to work became drudgery - each day harder and harder to face.

I didn't get the promotion – but someone less qualified did.

You know the story –Who You Know is the highest employment bid.

Then one day I heard that Dear Mother's voice speaking quietly,

She told me what God has for me – it is for me.

She said take life, baby, one day at a time.

Put your faith in God and you will be fine.

But as you know that is so easy to say,


We think we know what is best and still try to do it our way.

"Trust in the Lord with all thine heart," she said,

"He will direct your path. In my Father's house

There are many mansions, And sweetie, only what you do for God will last.

" What could I do but listen patiently?

She was right, what God has for me, is for me.

For years, my faith had been lacking-

that's why my life was a mess.

Trying to handle my own life had resulted in

that much more stress. This sweet loving

mother said take things one day at a time,

that trusting in God – my life would be fine…

Lean not to your understanding when things

don't go your way. Hold to His hand –

there'll be a brighter day.

Her trembling whispered voice went on and on…

it reminded me of my Grandmother's voice

and advice that came in scripture and songs.

What a Friend We Have in Jesus.

I Know My Jesus Cares. Child

He won't ever put on you any more

Than you can bear. Precious Lord, Take My Hand –

When Things Go Wrong.......Just Stand.

Finally I've learned I have a testimony – for every test

.....Worry will only age you, the same is true for stress.

I've learned to pray with faith knowing that

God hears me when I pray......

No matter how uncertain, illogical,

or hopeless life seems –God will show me the way.

## To Dad, With Love... Now I Understand

Maybe you weren't at every ball game

Maybe you missed that first touchdown

Perhaps you didn't meet my first date

Or show me how to skate...

...But now I understand...

At the time, I cried, I cursed, I moaned

With every disappointment I wondered how

Could you dare?

With time I've learned a lesson or two...

It wasn't that you didn't care,

You worked from morning to night

Making sure we were alright.

The bills were always paid

And the beds were always made.

We had clothes on our backs

When we needed something we just had to ask. I wanted you at every
outing,

If you were not, I'd do some pouting.

But now I understand that that

Was hard for you—now I understand you did what you had to do.

# Daddy's Tough Love

A Daddy's love is often a tough

love He disciplines and demands

When Daddy says yes or no

His decision usually stands.

His voice is strong, His manner stern

But neither is without care or concern.

Daddy's love is precious and abundant in his own way. Dads just have to be tough in raising children today.

He can't give his children to the streets,

Or leave them on Mother's doorstep

Even if he's "absent" his presence must still be felt. Yes, Daddy's love is tough love,

But love just the same...

Daddy's love is tough love....

But we love you just the same.

# We Don't Know His Plan

## But His Plan is to Prosper

# Us

# If For Brothers and Sisters

If you can trust where God has placed you,
In spite of ups and downs,
If you can force a smile some days,
When your heavy heart wears a frown.
If you lean not to your own understanding,
When others are putting you down,
If you will "fret not" when evil doers …
Do what evildoers do and call on God,
Knowing He will see you through.
If always it is the Kingdom of God
That you first seek…
If you can say a little prayer
Before you angrily speak.
If you can without hesitation
Turn the other cheek.
Remember, Jesus says blessed are the meek.
If you will judge not lest ye be judged,
And thank God for the little things,
Yes, the storms, snow, rain
And the sun shining high above.
If you can try to be forgiving when your
Heart's been badly broken,
If you've heard harsh words
from loved ones –

Words that never should be spoken.

If you can reach out to others,

When you see what they're going through,

Knowing you've been there, done that,

And the experience only strengthened you.

If you know He answers prayers,

If you know He's always there…

Then brothers and sisters keep on walking…

With your heads high in the air.

Don't let troubles get you down.

Don't let fear make you weak.

Fret not the evil doers.

And always the Kingdom of God

Always you must seek.

Keep stepping my brothers and sisters

If you know God is real,

Keep stepping with your head held high

Your joy no one will ever steal!

# Beginning Today – I'm Not Looking Back

*"Joy joy unspeakable joy, the world didn't give it to you and the world can't take it away." The world will try with Satan's urging, but the world can't take it away.*

Beginning today, I'm not looking back.
When stuff happens, and it will, you must
Lean not to your own understanding, but in all
Ways, acknowledge the Father
And He will, as He does, direct our paths.
Beginning today, I'm not looking back.
"You don't know the plans God has for you…plans for…
Beginning today, I'm not looking back.
When the bills come early
but the money comes late.
When every road you seem to travel
is more crooked than straight…
Take my advice, don't look back.
Pray a prayer that always works to
God who is always there…
"The Lord is my shepherd –
He puts no more on me than I can bear."
When the climate of your relationships
and friendships fall somewhere

Between fake and few, when those
who seemed like a friend
Were neither faithful nor true,
and you had to pray day and night.
For those who were spitefully using you... don't look back.
Remember, "If God is for you, who can be against you?"
Beginning today, I'm not looking back.
What about you??? I'm not looking back.
Beginning today, I'm looking forward... I'm looking up:
"I will lift up my eyes unto the hills
from whence cometh my help."
I'm looking inwardly: "If You find anything that
shouldn't be, take it out and strengthen me."
I'm looking confidently and faithfully:
"I can do all things through Christ, who strengthens me.
I'm looking prayerfully that my light will shine so that
"Others will see the works of the Heavenly Father."
I'm looking toward Heaven,
a time of continuous joy and peace,
a time of rejoicing and celebrating.
No more back-biting.
No more player-hating.
No more injustice. No more pain.
No more bought votes and borrowed time.
No more sadness. No more sorrow....
No hunger, no hate crimes...
Just joy. Unspeakable joy.
Beginning today. I am not looking back.

# When Satan Enters to Get You Off Center

Ever notice when things are going well,
You have peace of mind and
Life is "swell?
Somebody, somewhere initiates a sneak attack.
Then suddenly you're worried cause folks
who don't even know you….
are talking behind your back?
That's when Satan enters to get you off center!
Like those times when you hear
"He said, she said…"
And you get caught up too?
Talking about people that you know
have been good to you….
Adding to the story to make it sound better.
You know it's wrong but still the lies
you add get messier and messier!
That's when Satan enters to get you ….
Off center. Hold your ground. Take a stand.
Show Satan the sign that says
"Don't enter."
God is your joy.
God is your center.

# A Gracious Redeemer

My God is a Gracious Redeemer,
whose love is unconditional....
He forgives me of my sins
And says: "Child, don't even mention it."
He's my lawyer in the courtroom,
My doctor when I'm sick,
He's the Phenomenal One who molded me,
Shaped and made me unique.
He programmed my mind, gave me strength.
Put visions in my eyes.
I might not look like much to you
But God tells me I am "the prize."
And what do I do in return to please the Savior
for all that He does for me?
I simply pray to Him each day
and live so the world can see...
That He is the Redeemer, The Guiding Light,
The Master with the Master Plan....
Oh, I thank Him. I love Him. I praise Him.
He has the Whole World in His Hands.

# Will We Ever Learn?

Will we ever learn to be like Jesus?
Will we learn to forgive AND forget?
Will we learn to be there for others—
Jesus came as a living example…
But we haven't learned yet.

Will we ever learn that God
Is always available for us?
Will we ever learn that on Him and in Him
We can forever Lean and Trust?
Will we learn to simply call on His name?
Will we learn that being a Christian
Is no reason to be ashamed?

Will we ever learn that only what we do
For Christ will last?
Will we learn to be patient, to put God first?
And always give our best?
Will we learn to make sacrifices as Jesus
Sacrificed His life?
He died for us and what do we say –
"Oh, he did? That's nice???"
God is awesome, magnificent, wonderful,
Gentle, patient, reliable, forgiving,

Guiding light, a healer,

Protector, a shelter in the storm,

A provider, a bill payer, and a dragon slayer

…. Will we ever learn??

Will we ever learn to be there for Him

….As He is always here for us.

## Satan's Kids

Just lift them up and let them go,
They will pull you down that I know.
You won't see any horns, pitch forks, or pointed tails.
But they are Satan's kids, and they will give you hell.
Just lift them up and let them go.
Pray them up throughout the day,
As much as you can… stay out of their way.
They have a plan to take you down,
They will sneak up on you without a sound.
Just lift them up and let them go.
Keep praying for your own safety and peace
As often as you can –
Get on your knees.
Their job is to stand between you and Heaven.
Just lift them up and let them go.
Even when you think you have prayed enough,
Please, please just pray some more.

# As We Forgive Those....

*Forgive them Father for they know not what they do. Luke 23:34*

But some do Lord – they know what they do,
When they do the things they do,
They know what they say,
When they say the awful things they say,
Some know very well,
But if I don't forgive, that means
I'll be right there with them,
Suffering the Heat of Hell....
Bless them that curse you, do good to
them that hate you, and pray for them
which despitefully use you
and persecute you. Matthew 5:44
But Father, they know the suffering they cause
Some deliberately block my path – just to see me fall,
Am I to forgive them when the hurt is more than I can bear?
I've tried to forget, but painful reminders are everywhere.
Yes, You did it! You forgave – even from the cross on Calvary.
Am I forgetting now how many times You have forgiven me?
Forgive us our trespasses as we forgive
those who trespass against us. Matthew 6:12
I do hear you, Father, and Your Word is as clear as it can be.
If I don't forgive my brother or sister, why should you forgive me?

Yes, they know my sadness, my pain, my hurts, my sorrow.

But if I can't BE forgiving today....

You're right – how can I expect to SEE

You forgive ME tomorrow??

# It's Just You and Me Jesus

Nobody's shoulder to cry on,
And my shrink's out of town,
So I guess it's just me and you, Jesus,
Do you mind if I sit down?
I know I shouldn't have waited,
until the very last minute,
But somehow I thought things were under control
I thought that I could swing it.
But here I am, Lord, right back where I started,
Broken down, confused Lord,
with broken spirits, and yes, Lord, broken-hearted.
Yes, there were many times I could have
Turned everything over to You.
Instead, I talked to so-called friends
knowing full well there was nothing they could do.
So now I guess it's just me and you, Jesus,
You can pull me through this I know.
It won't even cost me a co-pay –
if I now just let go and let you handle my life,
and all my concerns.
It's just you and me, Jesus,
Many lessons I'm yet to learn.
Don't know why you're the last one I call on,

You're the first to do me right,

Seems by now I would trust and believe,

That through you all things are possible…

It is not my battle but yours to fight.

But here I am again Lord,

Begging for Your mercy, Your strength, Your guiding light

Praying that you'll lead me Lord.

I need you day and night.

# Still Surviving...

One would think that 40 years of trying to be just the right partner for just the right person would work. But it rarely does. People change. Circumstances change. Expectations change. And relationships change.

God continued to cover me through the discrimination, the growth, the paths set forth to simply move on. When He created me, He created Survival Spirit. He created in me a Keep-it- Moving Mindset. He created me from Don't-Give-Up-Now DNA. If my ancestors had survived the Middle Passage, and Jim Crow, Brown vs. the Board of Unequal Education, and Sit-Ins at Selma, and Bulldogs in Birmingham – surely, I could and would survive whatever was to come my way when I found myself between a rock and a very hard place.

In closing, I am today. . . still surviving. Still writing. Still feeling God's Favor and His Covering. Still finding myself too many times for comfort between that proverbial Rock and a Very Hard Place. But my Don't-Give-Up-Now-DNA is strong so whatever it is, whoever it is, wherever it is. . .it must know by now, in the words of Jerry Butler – Only the Strong Survive!!!

I hope and pray that along this very long journey I have learned the importance of forgiveness. People will hurt you... sometimes intentionally and sometimes unintentionally. But more than anything – I believe I have learned to love myself, trust God, Be Still and know He is God!

Just a simple reminder: No one knows the day or the hour, so live your life to the fullest. Help someone in need. Realize... you can't take it with you and God sees your every step and knows your every thought. Try to have joy no matter what goes on around you. As you are helping others, do understand not everyone welcomes your help and there really are some people you cannot help. Keep it moving. God will lead you to those open and ready to receive a blessing that He had just for them… But now if they are Satan's kids…. Ahhhh you might just want to keep praying them up.

In reading the book, The Four Agreements, I gained a new perspective: "everything we do is based on agreements that we make with ourselves, with others, with God and with life." To find personal joy we must get rid of fear for one. (Remember: Don't let fear interfere you're your faith!) We can transform ourselves to get rid of negative thoughts based on experiences in life. Those four agreements are "be impeccable with your word, don't take things personally, don't make assumptions, and always do your best." That sounds simple…If we always do our best the first three agreements are somewhat built in or are easier to accomplish. My lesson from this book is yes do my best and don't take things personally. That is my Survival Strategy.

With that said, trust me I have no other choice but to survive. If any of what I have shared, resonates with you - you too are surviving because you have no other choice. Yes, the poetry reads as if there is a lot of pain. Absolutely, I have suffered. I have had my joy taken. But I am back – full force – by God's Grace. A former pastor used to include in his messages that if you have never experienced pain in your life, you haven't lived long enough. We are all either going through something, just came out of something, or we are about to go through something. Matthew 5:45 says, "God causes his sun to rise on the evil and he good and sends rain on the righteous and the unrighteous…He lets rain fall on them whether they are just or unjust."

And Winston Churchill I am told, said, "When you're going through hell, keep going." And that is how we all Survive Life Between a Rock and a Very Hard Place!!!

The closing poem is important to share as many times as possible now because what I wrote in 1996, that poem -Ego, Money, Power and Greed - has become true. This is a world riddled with selfishness, ego, and greed for money and power. Even when I look at George Floyd's death – it was about power. When I look at the political landscape of America, it is about money, and power, and ego. When I look at the failure of our public educational area, it is set up for failure because as long as children are under-educated and under-prepared, there will be a working class, a class of menial, unskilled labor which will lead to hopelessness and helplessness. Yes…. Ego, Money, and Power.

# The Ultimate Sin – Ego, Money and Power

How could the people not know –
It keeps happening again and again,
a world running over with sorrow
A world running over with sin!
How could they not know?
That ego, money, and power would
Bring the world to an end?
As smart as man was, this he could not prevent.
He watched it happen gradually –
But was too ignorant to know what it all meant.
Oh, he brilliantly predicted stock market crashes,
Population booms and the weather.
But in all of man's "infinite" wisdom,
He never knew why people couldn't live together.
The answers weren't so complex
It didn't' take a rocket scientist to figure it out—
It's just that man knew so little about love.
He didn't know it was something the world
Could not do without!
Because man himself was hung up
On material goods and wealth.
He daily focused on ego, money, and power.
And what he could do for himself.
Oh, his IQ was "off the hook,"

He could pass all kinds of exams,
But his LQ was in the negative
The LOVE QUOTIENT was a sham.
Take the employer who could care less
About a single parent's demise –
He didn't care that her ends didn't meet –
That each week she was just getting by.
He ignored an associate's cry for help
The one that committed suicide,
He chalked it up to attrition and his man-made
Twenty-first Century Downsize!!
Concerned with ego, money, and power,
Some even fought in the church.
They didn't care who they hurt.
There were doctors in the world driven
By the patient's "ability to pay,"
It's no wonder that ego, money, and power
Would bring on the Judgment Day.
The lawyers had begun to sue one another
Using clients as their excuse.
If you look closely around you today,
You'll know I speak the truth.
Police who vowed to serve and protect,
Knew nothing about compassion or respect.
They were killing young people left and right,
And suspended with pay – oh what a sight!
How long would God let us carry on…
We'd lost all sense of right and wrong.
Ego, money, and power – greed everywhere,

people so self–centered, and way too busy for prayer.

What is missing? What is it we do not understand??

That we love one another is God's first commandment

He makes that clear for every woman and man!

When we fail to love we lie, steal and kill –

Even those chosen to lead cut dirty deals.

Because ego, money, power is what we're all about

And little do we know love is something we cannot do without.

Ego, money, and power in the White House, the workplace, the home…..

Ego, money, and power with no remorse for doing wrong.

Ego, money, and power instilled in boys and girls

and as "intellectually enlightened" as we were

We didn't see it coming…….That's right… the destruction of this earth….

And I tell you it was something!

A chaotic mess with folks trying to save their cars, homes, and boats.

But God just wasn't hearing it, as he issued His final report:

"You all amaze me," God said,

"You're a day late, a dollar short.

You should have listened centuries ago…

I said I'd come again.

But you were too consumed with the evils of greed

And failure to love became your ultimate sin!"

# About the Author

Dr. Regina Vincent-Williams is an author, poet, and transformational speaker who lives in Fremont, Ohio. In her spare time, she enjoys beekeeping/honey gathering, gardening, travel, and community service. Dr. Vincent-Williams is unapologetic in sharing her lived experiences and her faith in believing the following: God knows the plans He has for us (to prosper us) and secondly, what God has for you – it is for you! Email her for speaking engagements and workshops, at JCV Communications, Box 566, Fremont OH 43420 - *www.drreginavincentwilliams.net.* Contact her at drreginavincentwilliams@gmail.com.

www.ingramcontent.com/pod-product-compliance
Lightning Source LLC
Chambersburg PA
CBHW051528120626
46551CB00012B/1120